WORLD OF KNOWLEDGE
MEDICINE

BELITHA PRESS

This edition published in 2003 by
Belitha Press
A member of Chrysalis Books plc
64 Brewery Road, London N7 9NT

Typeset by Chambers Wallace, London
Printed in China
British Library Cataloguing in Publication Data
for this book is available from the British Library.

ISBN 184138 606 5

Acknowledgements

Photographic credits:

Bibliothèque Nationale 16
Bodleian Library 11 left
Bridgman Art Library 4 centre
J. Allan Cash 32
Mark Edwards 50 top
ET Archive 5, 43 left
Mary Evans Picture Library 13 bottom, 36 left
Werner Forman Archive 55
Format Photographers 50 bottom
Giraudon 25 bottom
Sally and Richard Greenhill 7 right, 38, 57
Robert Harding Picture Library 49
Hulton Picture Company 30 left, 33 right
Hutchinson Library 47, 48, 51, 52, 53, 54 right, 56, 58 left, 59
Imperial War Museum 33 left
The Independent 58 right
Magnum 4 left, 35 right, 42, 43 right
Mansell Collection 13 centre, 31
Massachusetts General Hospital 34

Master and Fellows of Trinity College, Cambridge 19 centre
National Portrait Gallery 25 top
Peter Newark's Western Americana 54 left
Österreichische National Bibliothek 17
Popperfoto 7 left, 35 top
Queen Mary's Hospital Roehampton 44 left
Ann Ronan Picture Library 13 left, 22 left, 27 top
Science Museum 10, 11 right
Science Photo Library 32, 37, 39 left, 40, 41, 43 top, 44 bottom
Ronald Sheridan's Photo Library 12, 14
John Watney Photo Library 19 top, 27 bottom, 30 bottom, 39 right, 44 inset, 45
Wellcome Institute 8, 21, 22 right
Windsor Castle, Royal Library © 1990 Her Majesty The Queen 20
Zefa 4, 9

Illustrated by: James Field, Borin van Loon and Eugene Fleury

Series editors: Neil Champion and Mark Sachner
Educational consultant: Carolyn Kain
Editors: Jill A. Laidlaw and Rita Reitci
Designed by: Groom and Pickerill
Picture research: Ann Usborne
Art director: Frances Mackay

Contents

Words found in **bold** are explained
in the glossary on pages 60 and 61

CHAPTER ONE

HEALTH AND MEDICINE

One Helps the Other

Health

Most people have good health most of the time. Good health is not just the absence of illness. It means both a healthy mind and a healthy body. People who eat a balanced diet and get plenty of exercise can fight disease better.

Illness

There are many things that can go wrong with the human body. People can get the measles, break a leg, or have a toothache. When

▼ Some of the fittest people in the world are the Nuba wrestlers from Africa.

▶ Right: In Queen Elizabeth I's time, it was pretty to be pale. Far right: Today, a suntan is thought to make a person look healthy, but the sun's rays can be harmful.

4

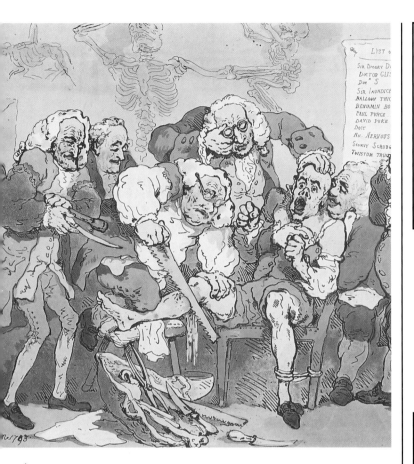

◄ The horrors of having a leg cut off are shown in this cartoon of 1793.

this happens, people usually need medical care.

Medicine

Since the beginning of time human beings have tried to cure themselves from illness. Even if the illness and its causes were unknown, medicines would be invented. Many medicines did no good at all but over the centuries we have discovered a great deal about our bodies and how to keep them healthy and how to cure them when they fall ill.

WHO's health

In 1948, the United Nations set up the World Health Organization – WHO. WHO wants to make sure that all people of the world are as healthy as possible. There are many WHO medical projects:

● Controlling diseases.

● Training doctors and nurses.

● Helping victims of natural disasters such as earthquakes, floods and hurricanes.

● Giving advice to countries about medicine.

Keeping Healthy

Taking care of yourself

Some people do not take care of themselves. They eat too much and do not exercise. They smoke cigarettes and drink too much alcohol. When they become ill, they do not go to a doctor straight away to seek help. When they finally do go to a doctor, they want to be cured quickly. These people may think: 'Why should I take care of myself? Medical care is so good that doctors can cure me.'

The cost of medicine

Modern medicine cannot cure everything. There are many

▲ Two different ways of taking medicine. Above – in North America and Europe, people simply open a bottle and take a pill that was made in a factory. Above right – in many other countries, people make their own medicines at home from plants.

diseases that have no cure. Also, medical care costs a great deal of money. Some people do not have enough money. In some countries health care is run by the government. Medical care is free at hospitals and surgeries because it has already been paid for in taxes.

Prevention is best

Where possible it makes more sense to stop illness before it starts. More and more people want to know how to take very good care of themselves.

When we need medicine

Not all illnesses need medical care.

● If you go to bed very late one night, the next day you might not feel your best. This does not mean that you are ill.

● If you have a sore throat and a cough, you might be a little bit ill. You will probably need to rest more than usual.

● If you catch the measles or the mumps, you are very ill. You will need to stay in bed and be given medical care.

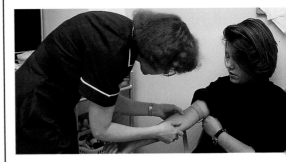

◄ Smoking was once thought to make people attractive. Today, smoking is known to be harmful to our bodies.

▲ A blood pressure check can warn a person if there is something wrong with his or her health.

7

Organizing Medical Care

In the past, people did not know very much about the human body and the things that could go wrong with it. There was little known about disease. Over time, doctors have learned more about the human body.

Today, medical care is organized into levels. No single doctor is expected to know

▶ Each society has its own form of medicine. A Chinese doctor checks his patient's pulse.

Spending on health

In the United States money spent on health care goes on childhood illnesses, diseases, mental illness, war veterans, and on health insurance for the poor and elderly.

▶ A class in anatomy during the Middle Ages. Throughout history, training doctors has always been a long process.

8

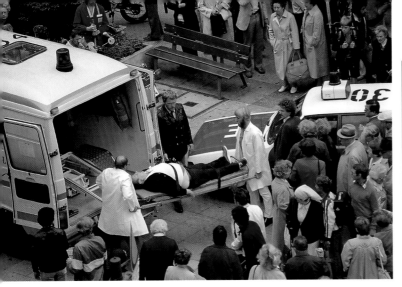

◄ Emergency care given by an ambulance staff.

Emergency!

When there has been a serious accident medical care is needed. Trained ambulance staff give treatment to the injured. This could be in the form of a fast-acting drug or a splint for a broken leg.

everything about all the different parts of the human body.

Primary care

Primary care means a trip to the family doctor. The family doctor knows his or her patients well. He or she can treat many common illnesses.

Secondary care

Secondary care involves specialists and hospitals. A specialist is a doctor who is an expert in a certain area of medicine. A cardiologist treats heart problems. An orthopaedic surgeon deals with bones, muscles, and joints. A pediatrician cares for children. People go to hospitals for things like **X-rays**, **blood tests** and operations.

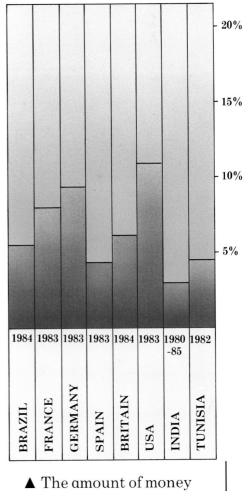

% OF GROSS NATIONAL PRODUCT

1984	1983	1983	1983	1984	1983	1980-85	1982
BRAZIL	FRANCE	GERMANY	SPAIN	BRITAIN	USA	INDIA	TUNISIA

▲ The amount of money governments spent on health care.

CHAPTER TWO
ANCIENT MEDICINE

The Start of Medicine

Medicine began when certain people became more skilled than others at taking care of the sick. Ancient skeletons show signs of broken bones that were healed. These bones were set (put back in place) by early doctors.

Trepanning
There are signs of the first medical operations. We have found holes in skulls that are over ten thousand years old. The holes were made during an operation called trepanning. The people of that time may have thought that this was a way of removing evil spirits. We know that patients

▲ A statue of Imhotep, an early Egyptian doctor.

► This ancient wall sculpture shows some of the instruments used in medicine in ancient Egypt.

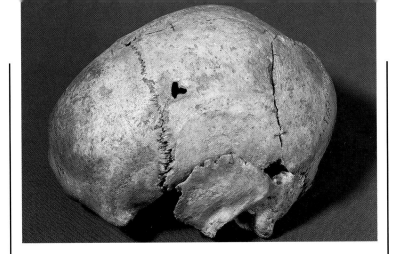

survived trepanning because they lived for years afterwards.

Ancient Egypt

About 4,600 years ago, the doctor Imhotep lived in ancient Egypt. People who were ill travelled long distances to be treated by him. After Imhotep died, people made him into a god. The sick worshipped statues of him in the hope of being cured.

The Egyptians put mouldy bread on their wounds. We know that a type of bread-mould can be used to make the drug called penicillin that heals wounds.

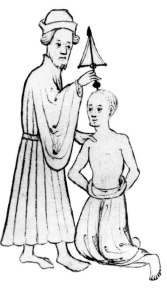

▲ Above, left: A 6,000-year-old skull with a hole in it made by trepanning. Above: The thong-drill was used to make the hole.

Early medical writings

Two writings were made on papyrus, a paper made from plants, about 3,500 years ago. The writings tell about medical care in ancient Egypt.

The Smith papyrus tells how to set broken bones, how to treat eye problems, how to stop bleeding and how to check a person's pulse.

The second document explains how to use about 900 medications. It gives chants and prayers to say to help cure certain illnesses. The papyrus also tells about special diets, massages and **hypnosis** to help people feel better.

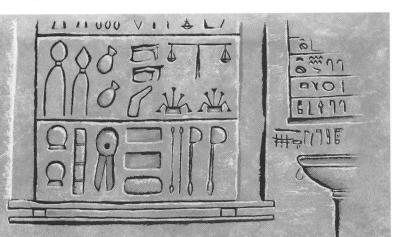

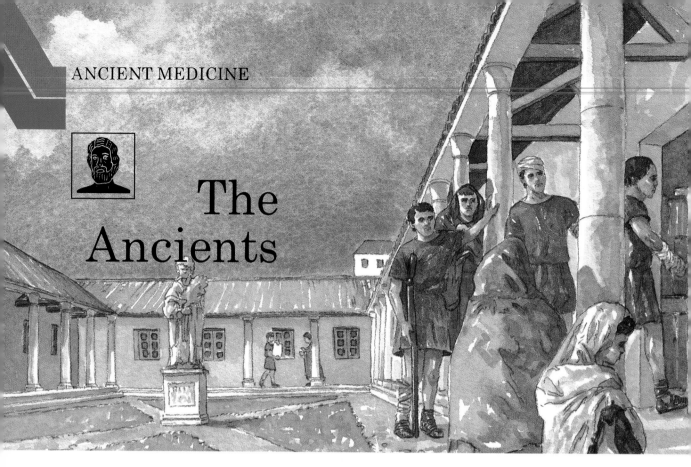

The Ancients

▲ Ill and injured people in ancient Rome could rest and recover in hospitals called *valetudunaria*.

▲ False teeth from ancient Rome. Dental care was only one part of Roman health care.

The ancient Greeks had a complex system of medicine. Alcmaeon (born about 535 BC) was one of the first people to cut open dead people for medical study. Empedocles (born about 492 BC) saw that the heart was connected to the blood vessels. Aristotle (born about 384 BC) made careful observations and experiments. He carefully noted his findings.

Roman advances

In the first century AD, Celsus wrote *De Medicina*. This was an encyclopaedia of Roman medicine. The Romans had the first hospitals. They built systems so that everyone had fresh, clean water. They also got rid of sewage. These things helped fight disease.

Galen

Galen (born about AD 130) wrote dozens of books about the human skeleton, muscles, nerves, brain and heart. His teachings make up the part of medicine known as anatomy. Anatomy is the structure of the human body and its many organs.

▲ Asklepios treating a patient in the 4th century BC. Ill people visited temples built in his honour where they prayed to be healed.

Dreams

Many priest-doctors worshipped Asklepios. A patient would go to one of his temples and sleep there overnight. In the morning, the patient would tell the priest about any dreams he or she had during the night. This would tell the priest what to do to cure the patient.

◄ Far left, top: Galen was a Roman doctor. He helped to start the study of anatomy. Far left, bottom: Empedocles, of ancient Greece, studied the heart and **blood vessels**. Left: Aristotle described and compared the parts of different animals. It was the beginning of the study called comparative anatomy.

The Father of Medicine

Hippocrates was a doctor, **surgeon**, scientist, and artist. He was born about 460 BC, on the Greek island of Cos. He was in charge of the medical school and hospital there. His writings and teachings helped to form much of our modern medicine.

In ancient Greece, religion and magic were a part of medicine. But Hippocrates and his followers believed that a doctor should examine the patient carefully to identify and work out treatment for the illness. They did not look for religious and magic

Founders of medicine

No single person was the founder of medicine. Hippocrates is famous but many Greeks and Romans helped.

'signs' as a cause of the illness.

Hippocrates believed that the body has amazing powers to heal itself when the illness is not too serious. Unnecessary treatment could make the patient worse.

The moral code

Hippocrates and his followers made guidelines about how doctors should think and act. They wrote that a doctor's main job is to help the patient. When a doctor gets personal information about a patient, this should not be told to others.

▲ Hippocrates as he might have walked through the medical school and hospital on Cos.

A balance

Aristotle believed in the four 'qualities' of life: hot, cold, wet and dry. These were added to the four 'elements': earth, air, fire, and water. If these were unbalanced illness happened. Later, illness was thought to be caused by the four 'humours': phlegm, blood, yellow bile and black bile.

The Dark Ages

CHAPTER THREE
MEDIEVAL MEDICINE

The Middle Ages or Dark Ages lasted from the 5th to about the 14th centuries in Europe. This period of time was called dark because there was little learning. This included medicine. The medical skills of the Egyptians, Greeks and Romans were forgotten. Yet in other parts of

The black death

The disease called bubonic plague, has killed millions of people. Between 1346-50, it killed 25 million people in Europe.

It was called the black death partly because bleeding in the skin made dark patches. This disease is spread to humans in two ways: by the bites of fleas that have sucked blood from infected rats, and by droplets coughed up or sneezed out by infected people. Bubonic plague can now be cured by **antibiotics** (see page 32).

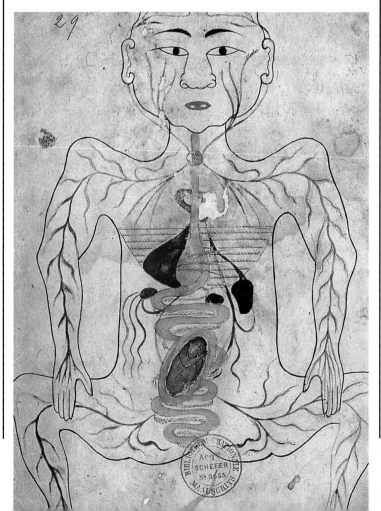

► This medical drawing of a pregnant woman was made for a Persian prince during the 10th and 11th centuries.

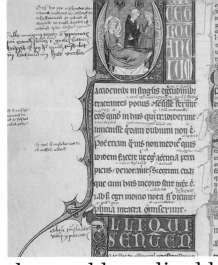

◄ A page from an Arabic medical book. It was translated from Arabic into Latin. Latin was the language spoken by educated people in Europe.

the world, medical knowledge was growing.

Famous doctors of Persia

In Persia, now Iran, a doctor known as Rhazes lived until AD 923. Rhazes wrote many medical books and gave one of the first descriptions of measles.

In the 11th century, a Persian doctor named Ibn Sina, wrote many medical books. His encyclopaedia, *Canon of Medicine*, became important in European medical schools for centuries.

Progress in India

In India, new medical knowledge about drugs and surgical instruments was becoming known. A doctor named Susruta rightly believed that mosquitoes spread malaria and that rats spread the plague (black death).

▲ Saints Cosmas and Damian, were famous for healing. Many saints were thought to have amazing healing powers.

Medicine and Religion

▼ Monks praying for the souls of sick people in the Middle Ages. They hoped to help ill people.

Throughout history, in many parts of the world, medicine has been linked with religion. From the 12th century, Christianity changed the practice of medicine.

For instance during this period, Christians viewed illness as being caused by spirits or supernatural beings. Herbs and medicines were used in treatment. The workings of the body were not as important as the soul. Prayers and offerings were made to cleanse the soul.

As a result of this type of thinking, scientific knowledge about the body became unclear.

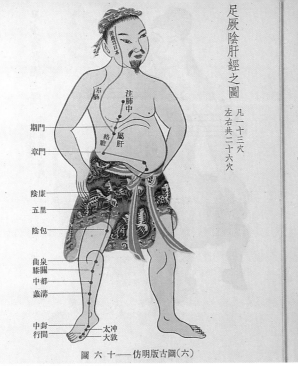

足厥陰肝經之圖

凡一十三穴
左右共二十六穴

圖六十一——仿明版古圖（六）

Medicine has often been confused with magic and superstition.

Eastern progress

Meanwhile, doctors in the East were learning more about medicine. In about 620-630, the Chinese doctor Chen Ch'uan was probably the first to study **diabetes**. In the 6th century, the Chinese wrote a large medical encyclopaedia describing over one thousand drugs.

◀ A chart of acupuncture points used in Eastern medicine (see page 49).

The Doctrine of Signatures

There are many stories, or myths, about the healing powers of plants. Some became included in what is known as the Doctrine of Signatures. This says that if a plant looks like part of the human body, it can be used to cure that body part. For example, lungwort leaves are rounded like lungs, so they were used for lung disease. The root of meadow saffron looks like a swollen foot, so it was used to treat swollen feet.

▼ This ginseng root looks like the legs of a human (see 'Doctrine of Signatures').

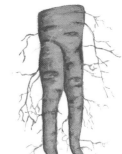

◀ Doctors and patients in a 13th century drawing. The patient on the left is getting heat therapy. The patient on the right has **leprosy**.

The Body Structure

▲ Constantine of Carthage translated Arabic medical works into Latin around AD 1050-80.

Art and anatomy

Leonardo da Vinci lived from 1452-1519. He was a great artist and scientist. He made many drawings of the bodies of humans and animals. But da Vinci's drawings were not published during his lifetime.

In the 3rd century BC, a Chinese medical book described human anatomy. In the 9th century the importance of anatomy was recognised by a famous Italian medical school called Salerno. It became part of every doctors training.

The Renaissance

During the early 14th century, the **Renaissance** began. Europe came out of the Dark Ages. Medicine made progress.

Great artists of the time, such as Michelangelo and Leonardo da Vinci, studied the human body

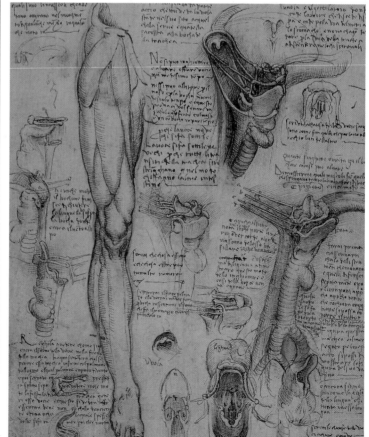

The Padua School

The Padua medical school in Italy produced many doctors.

● In the 1500s, Gabriello Fallopio studied the human body in detail.

● Santorio Sanctorius, born in 1561, began the study of body chemistry. He made an instrument to measure pulse rate.

closely. From their study of the muscles and organs, these artists made very accurate drawings of the human body.

The work of Vesalius

Andreas Vesalius was a professor of medicine in Italy. In 1543, he published a book called *The Structure of the Human Body*. Vesalius showed that in order to treat the human body when ill, doctors need to understand the body when it is healthy. With this idea, medicine entered a new era.

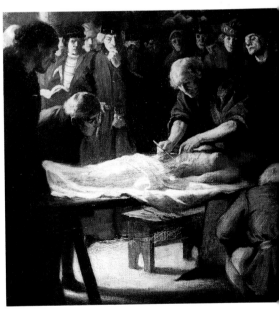

▲ Mundinus performs a dissection in Italy in 1318.

◄◄ Opposite: Leonardo da Vinci's anatomical drawings from a notebook.

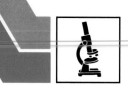

Looking and Learning

CHAPTER FOUR

SCIENTIFIC BEGINNINGS

During the 16th century, more and more medical knowledge became known. The printing press was invented and this made it easier for doctors to share their knowledge with each other. By this time doctors wanted scientific knowledge that was based on careful observation and experiment.

Fernel and Paracelsus

The scientific understanding of anatomy, physiology (organs and cells), and disease was increasing all the time. In 1554, the

Occupational diseases

Paracelsus recognized that a person's job could cause illness, such as a miner developing the disease of miner's lung. The Italian doctor Bernardino Ramazzini listed forty jobs that caused illnesses. This was the beginning of occupational medicine.

▶ Right: Paracelsus (1493-1541). Far right: Jean Fernel (1506-1588).

Frenchman Jean Francois Fernel wrote a textbook called *Universa Medicina*. It contained new information about medicine. It talked about human anatomy, physiology and new treatments.

About the same time, a doctor called Paracelsus was treating patients all over Europe. He gave his patients new drugs made of dangerous chemicals like mercury, sulphur, lead, iron, and copper. He also helped patients to talk about their illness.

▲ Ambroise (Andre) Paré was a French army surgeon from 1536-1545.

Germs

Over the centuries, doctors thought that germs might cause infections. In 1546, the Italian doctor Girolamo Fracastoro thought there were three ways in which disease might be spread: (1) by touching parts of the ill person's body; (2) by touching an object already touched by the ill person; and (3) by being in the same place as the ill person.

Medical Advances

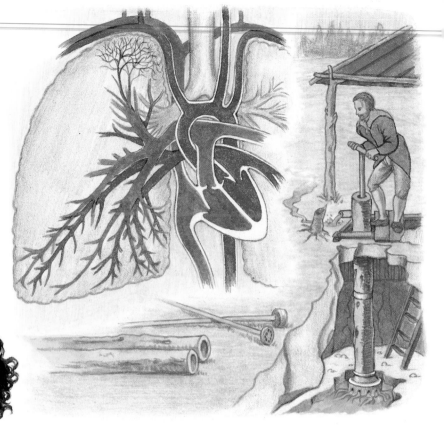

▲ William Harvey saw that new machines were being invented to pump water. He found that the heart pumped blood in a similar way to these machines.

▶ Opposite, top: Thomas Sydenham. Opposite, below: Pierre Fauchard.

Since Galen (see page 13) doctors had believed that the heart warmed the blood and that blood was made in the **liver**. They thought that blood seeped from **veins** to **arteries** through little holes in the heart's wall. Twelve centuries later Italian doctors proved that this was wrong but they could not discover what happened instead.

New discoveries
Over the next two centuries, more great medical discoveries were

made. These discoveries led to the medical practices in use today.

William Harvey (1578-1677)

In 1628, an English doctor, William Harvey, discovered that blood flows all the way around the body in only one direction. The heart has the job of pumping the blood.

Thomas Sydenham (1624-89)

Sydenham was known as the English Hippocrates. In 1666, he wrote a book called *The Method of Treating Fevers*. Sydenham believed that doctors should help to guide the body's own healing powers. His notes on the case histories of patients are still admired today.

Pierre Fauchard (1678-1761)

Fauchard was a French doctor who was the first person in Europe to suggest that the medical care of teeth was a speciality. The Chinese had been filling and capping teeth with gold for many centuries. In 1728, he wrote *The Surgeon Dentist*.

Medicine Branches Out

Edward Jenner (1749-1823)

Jenner was an English country doctor. His work was based on an idea that had been known in Asia for hundreds of years. He realised that by injecting a person with weak germs he could protect them from getting a more serious form of the same disease. He called this injection a vaccination. In 1796 his

vaccinations worked.

Thomas Hodgkin (1798-1864)

Hodgkin was interested in pathology, the study of diseased organs of the body. His work in the early 1800s helped make pathology an important part of medical science.

Louis Pasteur (1822-95)

In the mid-1800s, Pasteur showed that milk went sour because of tiny **organisms** (living things). He used this idea to discover ways to help prevent infections by germs.

Florence Nightingale (1820-1910)

Nightingale is the founder of nursing. She helped to care for British soldiers who were wounded in war. Florence Nightingale's dedication and skill soon led to new methods in nursing. She began the first nursing school in 1860.

Joseph Lister (1827-1912)

Lister made surgery much safer by trying to prevent infection in patients. In the mid-1800s, he was the first to use chemicals called **antiseptics** to kill infection.

Robert Koch (1843-1910)

Koch started the part of medicine known as **bacteriology**. He showed that certain things called **microbes** are the cause of many infectious diseases. In 1882, he discovered the germs that cause the disease tuberculosis.

Micro-scopes and Medicine

▶ Malpighi studies the structure of a frog. Because the parts can only be seen with a microscope they are called microscopic. Tubes that help the body to get rid of wastes are named Malpighian tubules after him.

Antony van Leeuwenhoek, a Dutch clothing merchant, had no scientific training. Yet in the 1660s he drew and described the red blood cells, muscle fibres and bacteria. He saw all of these tiny things under a microscope that he had made himself.

An Italian doctor, Marcello Malpighi, was the first doctor to

use a microscope. In 1661, while looking at a frog's lung under a microscope, he saw **capillaries**, the smallest blood vessels of all. Malpighi also studied eggs,

◀ Far left, top: Van Leeuwenhoek's first microscope, was hand-held. Far left, bottom: A later tabletop microscope by van Leeuwenhoek. Left: A modern electron microscope is so powerful it can see details of cells.

helping to form the science of **embryology**.

Medicine began to use the microscope more and more. This helped to diagnose and treat disease. In the late 1800s, improvements in the microscope began a new era in medicine.

The cell theory

By looking through microscopes scientists in the 19th century discovered that all living things were made of tiny units. They called these units cells.

Cells that go wrong

A doctor named Rudolf Virchow was certain that body tissues were made of cells. He thought that every cell in the body was made from another cell, sort of like building blocks. Virchow also believed that people get diseases when cells work wrongly or are being destroyed. These changes could be seen through a microscope. This was a new breakthrough. His ideas were the beginning of the part of medicine known as cellular pathology.

In 1900

CHAPTER FIVE

THE 20th CENTURY

In the year 1900, many new and important advances were made in modern medicine. The American doctor Walter Reed led a team that showed that the disease yellow fever was spread by the bite of a certain mosquito.

Scottish military officer William Leishman discovered that the tropical disease *kala-azar* was spread by sand flies.

▼ Frederick Banting and Charles Best with the dog they injected with **insulin** in 1921. Insulin became the treatment for the disease diabetes.

▶ A patient being helped by painting and drawing. This is called art therapy. It can help patients with mental or emotional problems.

Blood groups

Austrian doctor Karl Landsteiner showed that not all human blood was the same. He named the different types A, B and O. Later he found and named the AB type. In about 1940, Landsteiner helped to discover the Rhesus, or Rh, blood types.

Mental illness

At this time, Dr Sigmund Freud (also Austrian), worked to try and understand problems of the mind.

Medical teams

The era of the lone doctor making discoveries was ending. Doctors started to work in teams.

▲ Walter Reed making medical notes in his fight against yellow fever. In the background is the site of his research – the Panama Canal.

Modern drugs

In 1908 Paul Ehrlich (German) won the Nobel prize for medicine. He had studied the way the body develops resistance, or fights, against certain infections the patient has already had. He called this immunity. He gave children immunity against the throat disease diphtheria by injecting them with some of the germs of the disease. This method of fighting disease has saved many lives.

Wonder Drugs

▶ Alexander Fleming checks the growth of bacteria on a culture dish.

▼ Tropical swamps are home to the Anopheles mosquito. This mosquito spreads **malaria** with its bite.

In 1928, an accident caused one of the greatest advances in medicine. British scientist Alexander Fleming was studying bacteria in his laboratory. He was growing the bacteria on round dishes called culture dishes. A fungus carried in the air got into one of the dishes. As the mould grew, it killed the bacteria.

Fleming found that the mould made a substance which could kill several types of bacteria that caused illness. Fleming called the substance made by the mould penicillin.

Production and testing

The next job was to make pure penicillin in large amounts. Then the penicillin had to be tested. The first tests during World War II were successful. This was the beginning of the era of drugs called antibiotic drugs.

Antibiotics today

Today, there are dozens of antibiotic drugs. Some attack many types of bacteria. Some kill only a few types of bacteria. All of them fight illness.

▲ Jonas Salk examines bottles of organisms in his American laboratory in 1955. He developed the vaccine against the disease polio which cripples the body.

Did you know?

Malaria is one of the world's major diseases. In 1630 quinine was used to treat it. This is a natural substance from the cinchona tree. Since 1934, human-made drugs have been used against malaria.

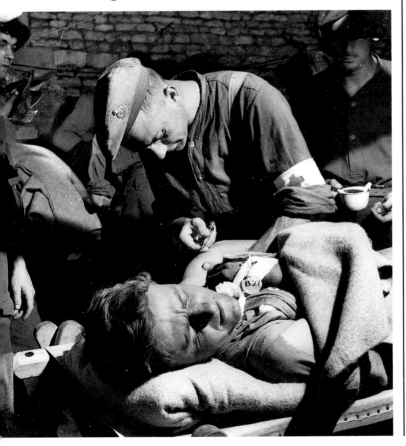

◄ Injured troops receiving antibiotics during World War II. This saved millions of lives.

Advances in Surgery

During the early and mid-20th century, improvements were being made in surgery. This was partly because of anaesthetics. Anaesthetics cause a loss of feeling or awareness in one part or all of the patients body, so the patient does not feel pain.

Anaesthetics

Early doctors gave their patients drugs to dull the patient's senses during surgery. But there were no drugs that would put a patient completely to sleep. This meant that surgery had to be performed very quickly.

▲ John Snow, a British anaesthetist, used this type of **chloroform** inhaler in the 1850s to put patients to sleep.

▶ Robert Hinckley's painting of American William Morton using ether as an anaesthetic.

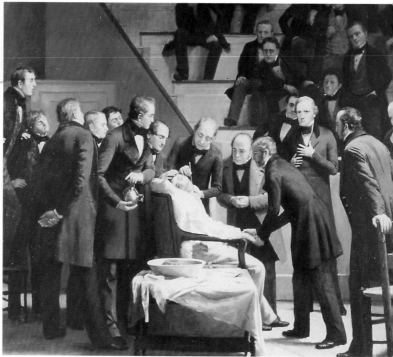

In 1845, an American dentist, Horace Wells, used the fumes given off by liquid **ether** to put a patient to sleep. In 1846, a doctor named William Morton operated on a patient's neck while the patient was anaesthetized with ether. Since that time, anaesthetics have become an important part of medicine.

Anaesthesia allowed doctors to take more time and care during surgery because the patient could not feel the pain of the operation.

▲ Top: Christiaan Barnard operating. Above: Barnard carried out the world's first heart transplant in 1969.

X-rays and Radiology

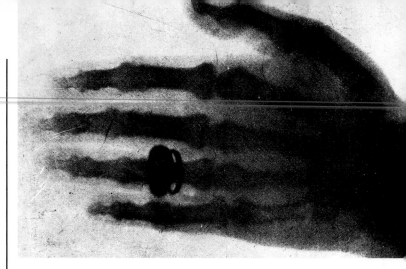

▲ Above, top: Wilhelm Röntgen's X-ray of his wife's hand shows her bones and ring. Above: Wilhelm Röntgen.

In Germany in 1895, Wilhelm Röntgen was experimenting with a device called the vacuum tube. He found that it gave off invisible rays that could pass through things like wood.

The first X-rays

Röntgen saw that the rays would pass through the body's flesh and

▶ An early X-ray clinic at about the end of the 19th century.

Did you know?

In 1896 the first patient to be helped by X-rays, had his broken arm set using the X-ray as guide.

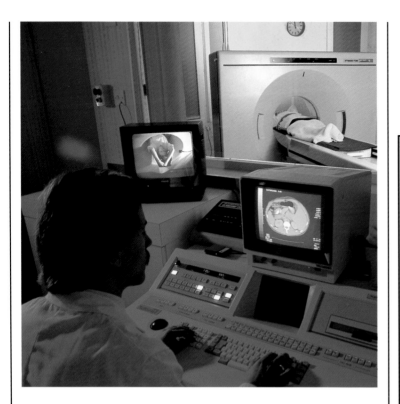

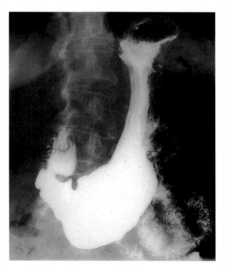

A CAT (Computerized Axial Tomography) scan in progress. The screen shows the lower part of the patient's body.

The dangers of X-rays

During the early days of X-rays, some people suffered from **skin ulcers**, **anaemia** and cancer. It was later shown that high doses of X-rays harm our bodies and bring on disease. Doctors turned this into an advantage by using carefully controlled X-rays to kill off diseased tissues such as cancer. This is known as radiotherapy.

muscle, but not through **cartilage** or bone. He took a picture of his wife's hand and made the first medical X-ray.

Doctors realized that X-rays could be used to see inside a person's body. This helped them find problems in the body and breaks in bones. In the early 1900s, a method was developed of making an X-ray of the stomach.

This new medical science became known as radiology. A modern part of radiology is called the CAT scan. It allows doctors to see inside a patient's body using X-rays and computers.

▲ An X-ray of the stomach. A substance called barium that the patient has swallowed outlines the stomach clearly in white.

Check-ups
and Tests

► People should visit the dentist every 6-12 months. The dentist looks for early signs of tooth decay and gum disease. If there is none then he or she cleans the teeth.

The quality of life

One aim of medicine is to help people live longer lives. Another aim is to stop suffering. These two things do not always go together. For example, a baby may be deformed. Many operations are needed to give the baby a chance to live. But it's quality of life may not be very good. An elderly person may have a serious disease that could be cured with treatment. But the treatment has painful side effects. Again, the quality of life would not be very good. Quality of life is not always helped by check-ups and tests.

CHAPTER SIX

MEDICINE TODAY

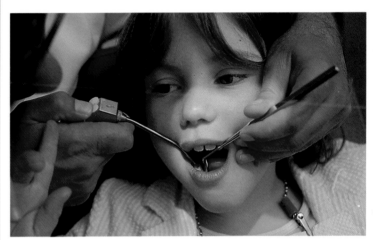

A check-up
Some serious conditions, such as some cancers and heart problems, can be seen in their early stages. Check-ups are usually done on people who doctors think are most at risk. People of a certain age who are at risk from a certain disease and people who have a family history of a certain disease should be checked.

A medical history
The signs of a disease or illness are called symptoms. When the patient visits the doctor they are

asked about the problem and their past illnesses. This is called taking a medical history.

Next, the doctor and medical staff may carry out what are known as diagnostic tests. These are tests such as a blood test or a urine test. These may tell the doctor what is wrong. Further tests may be carried out such as X-rays and scans.

◄ A CAT scanner reveals a brain tumour. The computer displays the tumour in green. This tumour can be taken out before it causes problems.

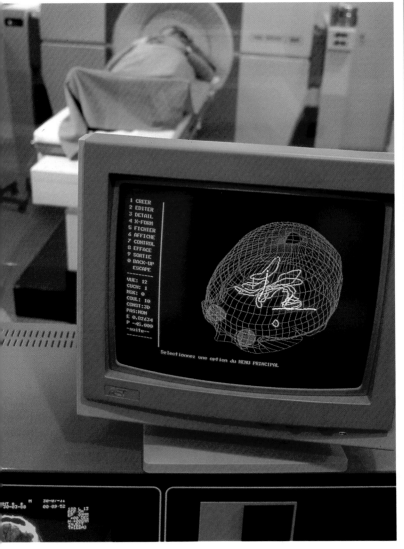

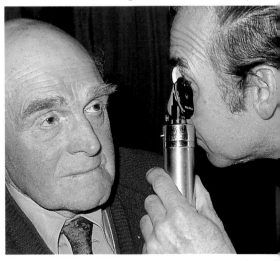

▲ Examining the eye can reveal high blood pressure. The doctor can tell this by looking at it's nerves and vessels.

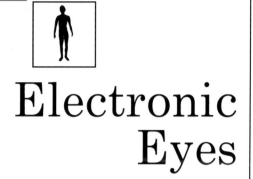

Electronic Eyes

▼ Below: Thermography takes the temperatures of body parts. Below right: Nuclear magnetic resonance (NMR) shows the body's response to a magnetic field. You can see the plum the man is eating.

With modern equipment, doctors can see in detail the structure and workings of the body without having to cut it open.

ECGs and EEGs

As the heart pumps, and the muscles pull, and the brain thinks, tiny bursts of electricity are produced. These bursts travel through the body. Problems going on inside the body can be discovered by electrical equipment.

The ECG, or electrocardiograph, shows heartbeats by measuring the heart's electrical signals.

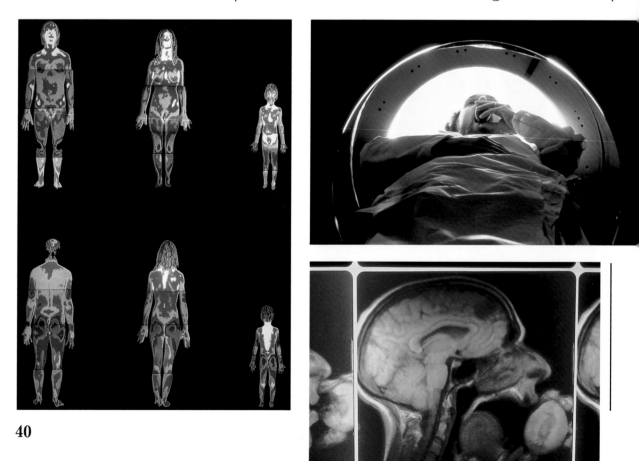

These signals tell a doctor if parts of the heart are diseased.

The EEG, or electro-encephalograph, detects electrical signals from the brain called brain waves. These brain waves can tell a doctor if the brain is not working normally.

▲ The CAT scanner is like an X-ray camera that goes around a person's body. The image that is made is very detailed.

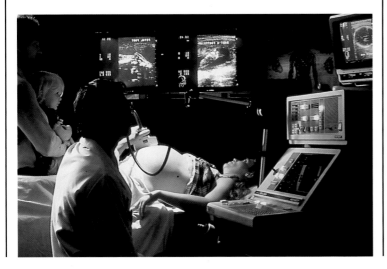

◄ This pregnant woman is having an ultrasound scan. High-pitched sound waves are sent through her body. The sound waves are then turned into a picture by the computer. Ultrasound helps to check if the growing baby is healthy.

MEDICINE TODAY

Drug Treatments

▼ Developing a new drug takes years and costs a great deal of money. Only a few of the many drugs tested pass all the tests and can be used by patients.

Prescribing drugs

Prescribing, or selecting, the correct drug for a patient is not easy. Many things have to be considered. It must be the right drug to act against the disease or illness. It must be the right dose, or amount, for the person. There must be no contra-indications. These are conditions that the patient has, or has had in the past, that would cause problems. For example, certain drugs should not be given to a patient who has **kidney disease**. Some people might suffer side-effects from certain drugs. Also, taking two different drugs together may cause problems.

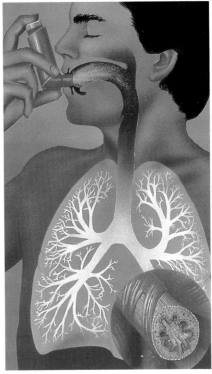

◄ Tests done on samples of blood, urine and other body fluids show how quickly a drug is used by the body. This can tell a doctor a great deal.

Drug safety

A new drug has to be tested. If the drug passes all the tests people can start to use it. Even so, problems with a drug can happen even after it has been tested. Sometimes this happens years after the drug has been in use. Then the drug is banned, or no longer prescribed.

▲ An inhaler for controlling asthma sends a drug into the body as a fine mist. This puts the drug into the lungs.

◄ An old-fashioned chemist, or apothecary's shop, was filled with minerals and parts of plants and animals. These were used to help cure illness.

Surgery and Implants

Surgery

Most surgeons specialize in one area of the body. The cardiac surgeon operates on the heart. The neurosurgeon operates on the brain and nerves. Many operations involve a surgical team. The team includes the main surgeon, assistant surgeons, the anaesthetist (see page 34), nurses and operators of special machines such as X-ray equipment.

Transplants

A transplant is when a part is taken from one person's body and put into the body of another person. The person who gives the

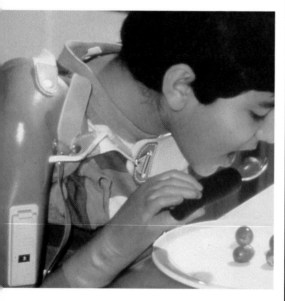

▲ This artificial arm is electronically controlled by muscles on the child's shoulder that can make it move.

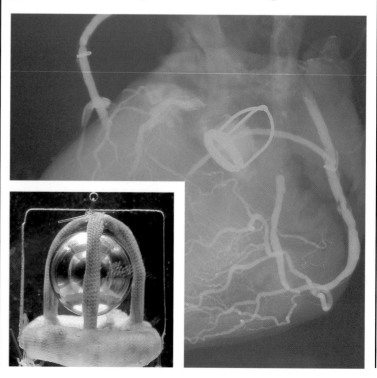

▶ An artificial heart valve and an X-ray showing the valve in place in the body.

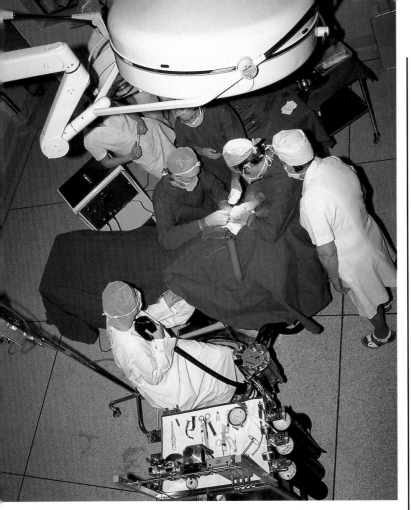

◀ The surgical team performing an operation. The anaesthetist is at the bottom of the photograph. The surgeons and nurses are around the patient.

Transplants and implants

1. Metal plate
2. Plastic eye
3. Rubber ear
4. Fillings
5. Jaw
6. Teeth
7. Voice-box
8. Lung
9. Arm
10. Pacemaker
11. Valve
12. Heart
13. Breast implant
14. Shoulder
15. Elbow
16. Wrist
17. Knuckles
18. Liver
19. Kidney
20. Pancreas
21. Insulin pump
22. Hip
23. Metal bone rods
24. Knee
25. Metal shin plates
26. Leg

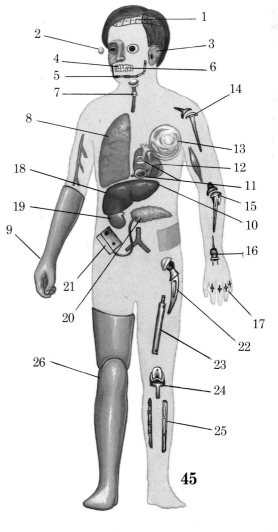

body part is the donor. The person who receives the body part is the recipient. Sometimes a recipient's body will fight against the transplant.

Implants

Artificial, or human-made, body parts are called implants. Implants, such as false teeth and glass eyes, have been used for a long time. Many new types of implants, such as artificial hips and knees, have been developed.

45

Treating the Mind

The ancient Chinese, Greek and Indian people knew that some illnesses are not caused by the body. Some illnesses are caused by the mind. Early ideas of mental illness were often linked to magic. For centuries people with mental illnesses were locked in special hospitals and forgotten.

The beginnings of psychiatry

In the late 19th and early 20th centuries, some doctors became

► Modern life has many stresses such as overwork and worries about family, jobs and money. Stress can lead to mental and emotional problems.

interested in mental illness. One of the first doctors who tried to explain mental illness was Sigmund Freud from Vienna, Austria. He studied how the mind works and why people act and behave as they do. Freud was involved in the early stages of modern psychiatry – the study, diagnosis and treatment of mental illness. He began the approach known as psychoanalysis.

There are still many different ideas about why mental illness happens and how it should be treated. This part of medicine is known as psychiatry.

◀ Sigmund Freud thought that people's worries are shown to them in their dreams.

China and the East

▲ The sign for yin and yang. Yin represents the 'cool' female and yang the 'hot' male side of human nature.

▶ Traditional plant medicines for sale in a street market in China.

CHAPTER SEVEN

AROUND THE WORLD

Chinese medicine is very old. The Chinese believe that health is based on the balance between opposite forces. These forces are called *yin* and *yang*. When the two forces are not balanced we become ill.

Traditional treatments in China work to try and get the balance back. They include treatments like acupuncture, massage, and healing exercises.

Barefoot doctors

One-fifth of the people of the world live in China. There are not enough fully-trained doctors to go around. But there are over a

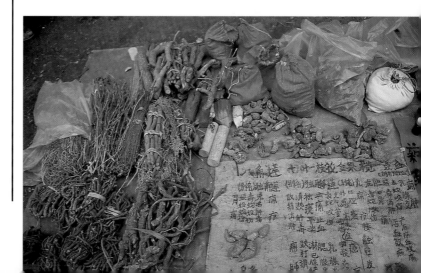

million part-time health workers who are trained (but not fully) in traditional and modern medicine. They are called barefoot doctors.

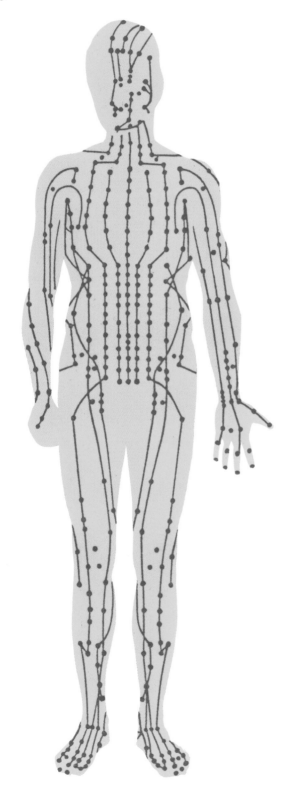

Medical facts: China

One way to know how good a medical system is in a country is to measure the life expectancy of the people. This is the average age to which people live. Another method is to find out the infant mortality rate. This is the number of babies dying just before, at, or soon after birth.

● In 1949, life expectancy in China was 30 years. In 1980, it was 68 years.

● The infant mortality rate in China is around 35 deaths per 1,000 babies.

◄ Acupuncture channels are said to carry energy through the body. Needles are put into the body to speed up or slow down the energy.

▼ Acupuncture is practiced in both China and Japan.

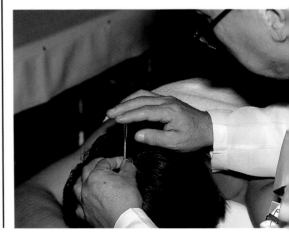

India and the Middle East

▶ Health workers in India tell people about family planning, or birth control. This is to stop people having babies that they cannot clothe and feed.

Medical facts: India

● Life expectancy for women is about 54 years; for men, 55 years.

● Infant mortality is about 110 deaths per 1,000 babies.

● Birth control is seen as an important way to reduce the population.

India and Pakistan

The traditional medicine of India is called *Ayurveda*. It is about three thousand years old. It is based on the use of herb medicines. Most Indian doctors are trained in both traditional and modern Western medicine. In Pakistan traditional medicine

▶ Shanty towns in India have open sewers and unclean water. Flies spread germs and disease.

◄ A man sells traditional plant medicines on a street in India.

▲ Some of Saudi Arabia's wealth has been spent on health care. This is the King Khaled Eye Hospital.

▼ The herb Rauwolfia has been used for more than 2,000 years in India. It contains reserpine, which calms the brain.

called *Unani-tibb* is practiced along with modern medicine.

The Middle East

Some countries in the Middle East have become rich from selling oil. They can afford modern Western medicine. Other countries in the Middle East are very poor. Their people have to live in dirty surroundings without proper medical care.

Africa

▶ A traditional diviner from Africa. She holds a special object that helps her to direct her spiritual healing powers.

▲ A traditional African healer, holding a bottle of medicine during a healing ceremony.

Healing by the spirits

Traditional medicine in Africa is practiced by people called healers. The healers know how to make medicines from plants. They know how to get in touch with the spirit world. The spirits pass their powers through them, so they are able to cure the sick.

Problems

The main problems that cause disease and illness in parts of Africa are poverty, lack of food and unclean conditions. Sometimes it is difficult for people to get medical care. They might not know where the medical centres are, or they may not be able to travel the long distance to get to the medical centre. Even if

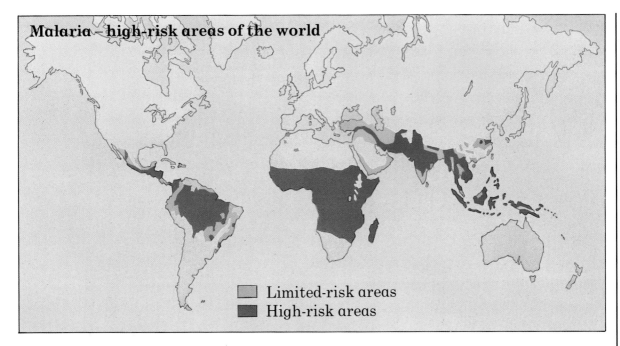

Malaria – high-risk areas of the world

Limited-risk areas
High-risk areas

▲ Malaria is one of the world's most serious health problems.

◄ These children of Ethiopia do not have enough food to eat. If they do not die of starvation then they may die of some illness that their bodies do not have the strength to fight because of lack of food.

medical care is available in their area, the people might be so poor that they cannot pay for it. Sometimes, people are not given care because of the colour of their skin. Governments that allow this to happen are racially prejudiced against their people.

Medical facts: Kenya

● Life expectancy for women is about 61 years; for men, 57 years.

● Infant mortality is less than 50 deaths per 1,000 babies.

53

The Americas

▶ This man from Ecuador grows herbs for medicine high in the Andean Mountains.

▲ The Mandan Medicine Man painted by the artist George Catlin in 1832.

North American Indians

For the Indians medicine is tied in closely with all of nature. The Indians want to live peacefully with the natural world and try to

save it, not destroy it. For example, the spirits might not be happy if an animal is killed at the wrong time. The Indians believe that the spirits would then cause illness in the tribe.

When a North American Indian became ill, the first person he or she went to was the herbalist. The herbalist told the ill person to take certain herbs, or plants, to be healed.

◄ A small statue made as an offering to the spirits by an Inuit (Eskimo) group in the far North of America.

Medical facts: Brazil

● Life expectancy for women is about 67 years; for men, 62 years.

● Infant mortality is less than 70 deaths per 1,000 babies.

Medical facts: Bolivia

● Life expectancy is 50 years. There are 120 deaths per 1,000 babies.

Did you know?

The massive spread of a disease is called an epidemic. An epidemic is often due to an illness being introduced to a new group of people, they have no resistance. In the 100 years after Europeans invaded North America, over 50 million American Indians died from diseases brought from Europe.

South American Indians

Like the Indians of North America, those in South America use herbs for healing. One famous group of South American Indian healers is the *Kallawaya* from Bolivia. Their name means 'carrying medicine on the shoulder'. They travel with bags of dried herbs, diagnosing and treating illness. Some Indian medicines are so effective that they are used in modern medicine.

The Coming Challenges

CHAPTER EIGHT

MEDICINE'S FUTURE

Each year, about six million people in the world develop a type of cancer. In cancers, some of the body cells go out of control. They multiply and form growths. They spread around the body. For many years, the causes of cancers were a mystery. But more and more cancers are being linked with the environment.

A new disease
In the early 1980s, a disease was recognized for the first time. It attacked the body's immune system. The immune system gives the body the ability to fight

Facts and feats
Smallpox has probably killed and disfigured more people than any other disease. In 1967, the World Health Organization began a fight against the disease with vaccinations. By 1979, the world was free of smallpox.

▶ Clean air, good food and pure water are necessary for health. The pollution of today will cause illness and disease for years to come.

◀ The foxglove flower (centre) contains a medicine that helps the heart beat more calmly and regularly. It was discovered by William Withering, an 18th century English doctor.

▲ Certain diseases run in families. Medical specialists can find out the risks for these people.

disease and illness. This new disease is called AIDS (Acquired Immune Deficiency Syndrome). It is caused by a virus known as HIV (Human Immunodeficiency Virus). AIDS stops the body's immune system working so that it can no longer survive illness.

A huge number of people have died from AIDS. Millions of people carry the HIV virus. The disease is expected to continue to spread at a very fast rate. Doctors are trying to discover drugs and vaccinations that will help in the fight against AIDS.

Success story

Many cancers are now being treated successfully. This is due to early discovery and better treatments. For example, in the 1950s only 1 child in 25 was cured of acute **lymphatic leukaemia.** By the late 1970s, it was 1 child in 2.

Healing the World

▶ These children in Romania have AIDS. They are living under terrible medical conditions. As yet, there is no cure for AIDS.

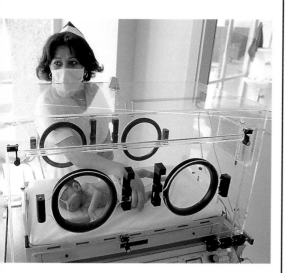

▲ In contrast to the Romanian children above, this newborn British baby is being looked after with great care.

The Future

People in the far distant future may look back and be puzzled about the medicine of today. They may wonder why we cut people open to cure them. They may ask why we struggled so hard to understand

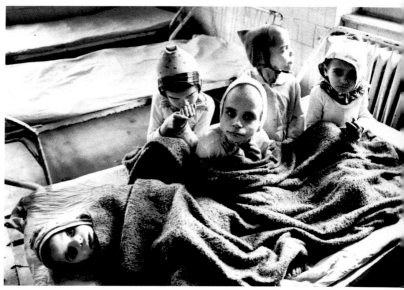

mental illness. They may wonder why millions of people in some parts of the world were dying of hunger, while others had more than enough food to eat.

Prevention is best

People need good food, clean water, and good living conditions. These things can help to prevent disease before it starts. Modern medicine helped to rid the world of the disease smallpox by 1979.

This was done through immunization. But this costs a great deal of money.

Progress

The progress of medicine depends on the research and discoveries of scientists. It also depends on how much money we are willing to spend. The modern world needs to keep aware of the importance of good medical care for all of its people everywhere in the world.

Holistic health

Some people say that medicine just treats a certain symptom or part of the body. Holistic medicine deals with the entire body and a person's mind, emotions, outlook, attitude and feelings towards life.

◄ Nature has supplied many medicines and cures. Yet in areas such as the Amazon rain forest, greedy people are destroying the plants and animals that could provide medicines. Perhaps many more remain undiscovered.

Glossary

Anaemia: an illness of the blood. It happens when a person does not have enough red cells. The sufferer looks very pale.

Antibiotics: a substance that kills off the viruses that cause disease.

Antiseptics: antiseptics kill **bacteria**. We clean our wounds with them in order to protect us from infection.

Arteries: arteries are the tubes that carry blood away from the heart around the body.

Bacteria: living things which can only be seen under a microscope. They are not plants or animals. Some are harmless but others cause infections and are called germs.

Bacteriology: the study of **bacteria**.

Blood tests: a test made on the blood which helps a doctor tell many things about the patient's health.

Blood vessels: tubes known as **arteries**, **capillaries** and **veins** that carry blood around the body.

Capillaries: tiny blood vessels that can only be seen under a microscope. They join small **arteries** to **veins**.

Cartilage: this is gristle. It is fixed to the joints in the body to strengthen and protect the bones and make movement easier.

Chloroform: a gas used as an anaesthetic to deaden the senses.

Diabetes: a disease in which too much sugar is found in the blood. This is due to a lack of **insulin**.

Diagnosis: finding out which disease or illness a person is suffering from.

Embryology: the study of the development and growth of babies in the womb.

Ether: a colourless liquid that is used as an anaesthetic.

Hypnosis: a sleep-like state of mind.

Insulin: a substance made by the body to control how sugar is used. If we do not make enough insulin then we have **diabetes**.

Kidney diseases: kidneys clean our blood stream. If they become diseased they cannot work properly and special machines have to do their job for them.

Leprosy: an incurable skin disease that causes total loss of feeling in parts of the body.

Liver: a large organ that does many things for our bodies like storing vitamins and iron and helping to digest fat.

Lymphatic Leukaemia: a cancer that harms the lymph gland. These are glands in the body that produce lymph, a watery substance that travels around the body collecting wastes, fighting infections and leaving nutrients.

Malaria: a disease in which a sufferer gets a fever (hot and cold sweats). It is caught by being bitten by certain mosquitoes usually found in hot countries. Once caught the disease can keep coming back.

Microbes: a word used to describe very small living things such as **bacteria** and tiny animals and plants.

Organisms: a living animal or plant.

Renaissance: a period of European history from the early 14th to the late 16th century. The name means rebirth and marks the change from the middle ages to the modern age. The rebirth refers to the revival of arts, literature, politics, trade, science and medicine.

Skin ulcers: open sores on the surface of the skin.

Smallpox: a disease that is easily passed on and involves fevers. One of its effects is boil-like marks appearing all over the skin.

Surgeon: a doctor who performs surgical operations is called a surgeon. In surgery the body is cut open and the diseased part of the body taken out or treated.

Veins: veins are tubes that carry blood to the heart from the rest of the body.

X-ray: discovered by Röntgen in 1895. A way of seeing bones inside the body by passing an invisible form of radiation through the body.

Index

A number in **bold** shows the entry is illustrated on that page. The same page often has writing about the entry too.